Bitcoin Unlocked:

The Ultimate Guide to Navigating the Future of Money

Bitcoin Unlocked: The Ultimate Guide to Navigating the Future of Money.

Table of Contents

Chapter 1: Introduction to Bitcoin

Bitcoin has captured the world's attention as a revolutionary form of digital currency. It's an asset that is both fascinating and complex, with the power to disrupt traditional financial systems, influence governments, and change the way individuals think about money.

What is Bitcoin?

Bitcoin is a decentralized digital currency, meaning it operates without a central authority, such as a government or financial institution. It allows people to exchange value directly without needing an intermediary. Unlike traditional currencies issued by central banks, Bitcoin is powered by a unique technology called *blockchain*, which records every transaction in a secure, distributed ledger across a network of computers worldwide.

Bitcoin was created in 2009 by an anonymous individual or group known as *Satoshi Nakamoto*. Since then, it has become the leading cryptocurrency, a new type of currency that exists only in digital form. Bitcoin has risen from an experimental asset used by a small community to a mainstream topic of interest for investors, technologists, economists, and even governments.

Why Bitcoin is Trending Now

Several factors have propelled Bitcoin to the forefront of finance and technology discussions worldwide. These include:

1. Financial Freedom and Control
○   Bitcoin allows individuals to have complete control over their money without relying on banks or governments. This independence appeals to people in regions with limited financial services or unstable economies.
2. Rising Concerns about Traditional Finance
○   Many people view Bitcoin as a hedge against inflation and the potential instability of traditional currencies. With some governments printing more money than ever, Bitcoin's fixed supply (only 21 million bitcoins will ever exist) attracts those seeking a "hard" asset that could retain value over time.
3. Technological Innovation
○   Bitcoin introduced groundbreaking concepts, such as blockchain, which have since been adopted for various applications beyond currency, from supply chain management to secure voting systems.
4. Global Accessibility
○   Bitcoin can be sent or received by anyone with an internet connection, making it a valuable tool in a world where access to financial services is not universal. With Bitcoin, individuals

are no longer restricted by borders, banking hours, or costly fees.

Purpose and Goals of This Guide

This book aims to demystify Bitcoin and give you a clear understanding of how it works, why it's significant, and how to navigate the world of Bitcoin effectively. *Bitcoin Unlocked* is structured to provide readers with foundational knowledge, as well as more advanced insights into Bitcoin's potential to reshape the financial world.

In the chapters that follow, you will learn about:

●   Bitcoin's Origins and Technology: The story behind Bitcoin's creation and the core principles of blockchain technology.
●   How Bitcoin Works: From transaction verification to mining, you'll understand the mechanics that make Bitcoin secure and functional.
●   Investment and Use Cases: Practical advice on buying, storing, and potentially profiting from Bitcoin.
●   Future Potential and Challenges: Bitcoin's role in the future financial landscape, including possible regulatory and environmental hurdles.

Why Read This Book?

Bitcoin is a fast-evolving technology with the potential to influence many aspects of daily life, from personal finance to global trade. Whether you're a beginner curious about what Bitcoin is or an investor considering adding Bitcoin to your portfolio, this book is designed to provide a balanced, practical overview of Bitcoin's possibilities.

You'll gain insights into:

●   How Bitcoin differs from traditional currency.
●   Practical steps to buy, store, and secure Bitcoin.
●   Ways Bitcoin could transform the future of finance.

With this guide, you're about to embark on a journey to understand one of the most intriguing financial and

technological developments of our time. Let's unlock Bitcoin's
secrets together!

Chapter 2: The Origins of Bitcoin

Bitcoin's story begins with the mysterious figure known as
Satoshi Nakamoto, who, in 2008, published a whitepaper titled
Bitcoin: A Peer-to-Peer Electronic Cash System. This document laid
out the blueprint for Bitcoin—a digital currency free from the
control of governments and banks. By January 2009, Nakamoto
released the first Bitcoin software, marking the birth of the
first decentralized cryptocurrency.

Key Milestones in Bitcoin's History

1.   The Genesis Block (2009):
o   Nakamoto mined the first-ever Bitcoin block, known as the
"Genesis Block" or "Block 0." This block contained a hidden
message: *"The Times 03/Jan/2009 Chancellor on brink of second
bailout for banks"*, hinting at Bitcoin's purpose as an
alternative to traditional financial systems.
2.   The First Bitcoin Transaction:
o   In May 2010, a programmer named Laszlo Hanyecz made history
by buying two pizzas for 10,000 bitcoins—a transaction worth
millions today. This purchase marked Bitcoin's first practical
use case and became a notable point of reference in Bitcoin's
timeline.

3.   Growing Adoption and the Emergence of Exchanges:
○   As more people learned about Bitcoin, it gained traction as both a currency and an asset. In 2011, Bitcoin reached parity with the U.S. dollar. Shortly after, cryptocurrency exchanges like Mt. Gox emerged, providing a place to trade Bitcoin for traditional currencies.
4.   Bitcoin as "Digital Gold":
○   By the mid-2010s, Bitcoin gained a reputation as "digital gold," a form of currency that could store value, similar to precious metals. This perception continues to attract investors who see Bitcoin as a hedge against economic uncertainty.

Bitcoin's origins are both revolutionary and enigmatic. While Nakamoto's identity remains unknown, Bitcoin's journey has been transformative, inspiring a movement that challenges the very structure of global finance.

Chapter 3: Understanding Blockchain Technology

Blockchain is the technological foundation of Bitcoin, a decentralized and transparent ledger that records every Bitcoin transaction. Understanding blockchain is essential to comprehending how Bitcoin works and why it's secure.

What is Blockchain?

A blockchain is a distributed database that stores data across a network of computers (nodes). Each "block" contains transaction data, a timestamp, and a link to the previous block, forming a "chain" of information. This design makes it nearly impossible to alter a transaction once it's recorded, as changing one block would require altering all subsequent blocks across the network— a feat that's practically unachievable.

Key Features of Blockchain Technology

1. Decentralization:
○   Unlike traditional databases managed by central authorities, blockchain operates across a network of computers. No single entity controls the data, making blockchain a decentralized and transparent system.
2. Immutability:
○   Once a transaction is recorded in a blockchain, it cannot be changed. This immutability ensures a high level of trust in the data, as no one can retroactively alter records.
3. Transparency:

○   Blockchain data is visible to anyone with network access. In the case of Bitcoin, every transaction can be viewed publicly, although users' identities are pseudonymous, represented by wallet addresses.

How Blockchain Powers Bitcoin

Blockchain's structure enables Bitcoin to function as a secure, decentralized currency. By eliminating the need for a central bank or third-party verifier, blockchain allows users to transact directly, with the assurance that transactions are valid and secure. This system not only empowers users but also reduces transaction fees, making Bitcoin an attractive alternative to traditional financial systems.

Blockchain technology has applications beyond Bitcoin, from supply chain management to secure voting systems, but its most groundbreaking role remains its impact on finance. For Bitcoin, blockchain is the core innovation that allows it to operate as a truly independent currency.

Chapter 4: How Bitcoin Works

Bitcoin is more than just digital money; it operates on a decentralized network with unique mechanisms for transaction validation and security. This chapter explains Bitcoin's inner workings, from peer-to-peer transactions to the role of miners.

Peer-to-Peer Transactions

At its core, Bitcoin enables peer-to-peer transactions. This means users can transfer Bitcoin directly to one another without needing an intermediary like a bank. This setup reduces transaction fees, increases speed, and allows for a global currency that's accessible anywhere with an internet connection.

Transaction Verification and Mining

Bitcoin transactions are verified through a process known as *mining*. Here's how it works:

1.   Nodes and Miners:
○   Bitcoin's network consists of thousands of computers, or *nodes*, that verify transactions. Special nodes, called *miners*, compete to solve complex mathematical problems, known as cryptographic hashes.
2.   Proof of Work:
○   To add a transaction block to the blockchain, miners must solve a mathematical puzzle. This process, known as *proof of work*, ensures that each block added to the chain is valid.
3.   Rewards and Security:
○   Miners are rewarded with newly created bitcoins and transaction fees. This incentive model keeps the network secure, as miners are financially motivated to maintain its integrity.

Public and Private Keys

Bitcoin relies on cryptographic keys for security:

● Public Key: The public key, or Bitcoin address, is where others can send Bitcoin.
● Private Key: The private key is a secret code that allows you to access and control your Bitcoin. Keeping it secure is essential because losing it means losing access to your Bitcoin.

Bitcoin Wallets

A *wallet* is a software or hardware device that stores your Bitcoin and private keys. Wallets come in various forms:

1. Hardware Wallets: Physical devices that store keys offline, providing a high level of security.
2. Software Wallets: Applications accessible on mobile or desktop, offering convenience but requiring strong security practices.
3. Paper Wallets: Printed documents with public and private keys, suitable for long-term storage but with limited usability.

Wallet security is critical. Many users adopt practices like enabling two-factor authentication and backing up their wallets to ensure they don't lose access.

Chapter 5: The Economics of Bitcoin

Bitcoin's unique economic model sets it apart from traditional currencies and assets. Understanding the underlying principles of Bitcoin's value, supply constraints, and volatility is crucial for anyone looking to engage with or invest in Bitcoin.

Bitcoin's Limited Supply

Bitcoin's supply is capped at 21 million coins, a feature coded into its protocol by its creator, Satoshi Nakamoto. This scarcity is a deliberate design to make Bitcoin deflationary, unlike traditional currencies, which can be printed at will by governments.

1. Halving Events:
○ Approximately every four years, the reward given to miners for validating transactions is halved in an event known as a *halving*. This reduces the rate at which new Bitcoin enters circulation, further increasing its scarcity over time.
○ Halving events often lead to increased demand and, subsequently, price surges, as they signal a slowdown in supply growth.
2. Digital Scarcity and Value Perception:
○ Similar to precious metals like gold, Bitcoin's scarcity has made it an attractive store of value. Many investors see it as a hedge against inflation, viewing Bitcoin as "digital gold."

Volatility: Why Bitcoin's Price Fluctuates

Bitcoin's price is famously volatile, swinging up and down with market news, investor sentiment, and macroeconomic conditions. Key factors include:

• Market Sentiment: News about regulatory changes, technological advancements, or major institutional investments can lead to sharp price movements.
• Liquidity: Bitcoin's market is still relatively small compared to traditional assets, meaning fewer large trades can influence its price.
• Speculative Nature: Many investors buy Bitcoin with the hope that its price will rise, leading to speculative trading and higher volatility.

Bitcoin as an Alternative to Fiat Money

Bitcoin's decentralized nature makes it an appealing alternative to fiat currencies, especially in regions with high inflation or unstable governments. In countries where the value of local currency is eroding rapidly, Bitcoin offers a way to preserve wealth without relying on traditional banks or financial institutions.

By understanding Bitcoin's economics, readers can better appreciate its value proposition and the unique factors influencing its price. This knowledge will help them make informed decisions about whether and when to invest in Bitcoin.

Chapter 6: How to Buy, Sell, and Store Bitcoin

Once readers understand Bitcoin's fundamentals, they'll want to know how to acquire, store, and secure it. This chapter provides practical, step-by-step guidance on entering the world of Bitcoin safely.

Where and How to Buy Bitcoin Safely

Bitcoin can be purchased on cryptocurrency exchanges, which act as marketplaces where buyers and sellers trade Bitcoin and other digital assets. Here's how to get started:

1.   Choose a Reputable Exchange:
○   Popular exchanges like Coinbase, Binance, and Kraken offer secure platforms for buying and trading Bitcoin. Look for exchanges with strong security features, transparent fee structures, and positive user reviews.
2.   Create an Account and Verify Identity:
○   Most exchanges require users to create an account and verify their identity for security and regulatory compliance.
3.   Buy Bitcoin:
○   Once verified, users can buy Bitcoin using various payment methods, such as bank transfers, credit cards, or even peer-to-peer transfers. Note that different payment methods may incur different fees.

Types of Bitcoin Wallets

To store Bitcoin securely, users need a wallet. There are different types of wallets, each with its own pros and cons.

1.   Hot Wallets (Software Wallets):
○   Hot wallets are connected to the internet and include mobile apps, desktop wallets, and web-based wallets. They are convenient for frequent transactions but are more vulnerable to cyberattacks.
2.   Cold Wallets (Hardware Wallets):
○   Cold wallets are offline devices, like Ledger or Trezor, that store Bitcoin safely. They are ideal for long-term storage and offer enhanced security.
3.   Paper Wallets:
○   A paper wallet is a printed piece of paper with a Bitcoin address and private key. While secure from hacking, it's less practical for regular use and can be lost or damaged.

Storing Bitcoin Securely: Best Practices

●   Enable Two-Factor Authentication (2FA): For exchanges and hot wallets, 2FA provides an additional security layer.
●   Use Strong, Unique Passwords: Avoid using simple passwords or reusing passwords across accounts.
●   Backup Wallets: Ensure wallet backup phrases or private keys are stored securely. This will be essential for recovery if devices are lost.

Selling Bitcoin

Selling Bitcoin is straightforward on most exchanges. Users can place a sell order on their chosen platform, specify the amount, and receive fiat currency or another cryptocurrency in return. The process can vary depending on the platform, with some offering instant sell options and others requiring waiting periods.

By following these steps, readers can safely buy, store, and protect their Bitcoin investments, reducing the risk of loss or theft.

Chapter 7: Bitcoin and the Broader Cryptocurrency Market

Bitcoin may be the first and most well-known cryptocurrency, but it's far from the only one. This chapter introduces readers to the broader cryptocurrency market, highlighting the differences between Bitcoin and other digital assets.

Comparison Between Bitcoin and Altcoins

1. Ethereum (ETH):
   o Ethereum is the second-largest cryptocurrency by market cap, but it differs from Bitcoin in that it's primarily a platform for decentralized applications (DApps) and smart contracts.
   o Unlike Bitcoin, Ethereum doesn't have a fixed supply, and its blockchain is optimized for programmability rather than just transactions.
2. Litecoin (LTC):
   o Created as a "lighter" version of Bitcoin, Litecoin features faster block generation times and a higher supply limit. It's often viewed as a testbed for new technologies that may later be implemented in Bitcoin.
3. Ripple (XRP):

o   Ripple is a cryptocurrency designed for quick, low-cost international payments. Unlike Bitcoin, which is decentralized, Ripple's development and issuance are overseen by the Ripple company, making it a more centralized asset.

Pros and Cons of Investing in Bitcoin vs. Other Cryptocurrencies

- Bitcoin:
o   Pros: Proven track record, large community, first-mover advantage, and recognition as "digital gold."
o   Cons: Slower transaction speeds and higher fees compared to some newer cryptocurrencies.
- Altcoins:
o   Pros: Many altcoins offer unique features and innovations, like faster transactions or programmable contracts.
o   Cons: Altcoins are often more volatile, less tested, and more susceptible to regulatory scrutiny or failure.

Bitcoin's Role as a Market Leader

Bitcoin's status as the first cryptocurrency gives it a special role in the market. Its value often sets the tone for other cryptocurrencies, and it is the most widely accepted and trusted among digital assets. However, the emergence of altcoins has diversified the market, offering users and investors more options and opportunities for specialized use cases.

Chapter 8: Legal and Regulatory Landscape

Bitcoin's decentralized and global nature poses challenges for regulators worldwide. Governments have responded in various ways, ranging from enthusiastic support to outright bans. This chapter explores the regulatory landscape, providing readers with an understanding of Bitcoin's legal status and potential implications for its future.

How Governments View Bitcoin Globally

The regulatory approach to Bitcoin varies widely across countries. Here's a breakdown of some key regions:

1. United States:
○   In the U.S., Bitcoin is classified as a property by the IRS, meaning it is subject to capital gains tax when sold. The SEC also monitors initial coin offerings (ICOs) and certain crypto assets, classifying some as securities.
2. European Union:
○   The EU has adopted a relatively open approach, though member states have varying regulations. The EU has focused on Anti-Money Laundering (AML) regulations, requiring exchanges to comply with identity verification standards.
3. Asia:
○   Japan is one of the most Bitcoin-friendly countries, recognizing Bitcoin as legal tender. China, on the other hand, has imposed strict bans on cryptocurrency exchanges and mining, although ownership remains technically legal.
4. Other Regions:

- El Salvador made headlines by adopting Bitcoin as legal tender in 2021, making it the first country to do so. Other countries, like India, have considered bans but have not implemented formal restrictions.

Current Regulations and Tax Implications

Most countries require Bitcoin transactions and profits to be reported for tax purposes. For example:

- Capital Gains Tax: Many countries tax Bitcoin profits as capital gains, meaning that investors owe taxes when they sell Bitcoin for a profit.
- Income Tax: In some cases, receiving Bitcoin as payment may be taxed as income. Bitcoin mining rewards are also often classified as taxable income.

Future of Regulation: Potential Impacts on Bitcoin's Growth

Bitcoin's growth has spurred calls for comprehensive regulation, particularly regarding its use in money laundering, tax evasion, and fraud. Increased regulation may bring both challenges and benefits:

- Challenges: Excessive regulation may restrict Bitcoin's use, making it difficult for companies and individuals to adopt or transact in Bitcoin.
- Benefits: Clear regulations may reduce uncertainty and encourage institutional adoption, helping Bitcoin achieve greater legitimacy in the financial system.

Understanding the regulatory landscape is crucial for anyone interested in Bitcoin, as legal developments could influence its future trajectory and adoption. While regulations may pose challenges, they could also legitimize Bitcoin, opening up new opportunities for growth.

Chapter 9: Bitcoin as an Investment

Bitcoin's reputation as a speculative asset has attracted the attention of both individual and institutional investors. This chapter explores Bitcoin's role as an investment, covering common strategies, risks, and rewards.

Different Investment Strategies

1.   HODLing:
○   The term *HODL* (Hold On for Dear Life) originated as a meme but has become a popular investment strategy. HODLing involves buying Bitcoin and holding it long-term, regardless of price fluctuations. This strategy is based on the belief that Bitcoin's value will increase over time as adoption grows.
2.   Trading:
○   Some investors choose to trade Bitcoin, buying and selling it to capitalize on short-term price movements. This requires a high level of knowledge, as Bitcoin's volatility can result in both high profits and significant losses.
3.   Dollar-Cost Averaging (DCA):
○   DCA is a strategy in which an investor buys a fixed amount of Bitcoin at regular intervals, regardless of price. This approach reduces the risk associated with market timing and allows for gradual accumulation over time.

Risks and Rewards of Investing in Bitcoin

●   Rewards: Bitcoin's scarcity, potential for high returns, and increasing institutional adoption have made it an attractive investment. Investors view it as a hedge against inflation and economic uncertainty.
●   Risks: Bitcoin is highly volatile, with frequent price swings that can result in significant losses. Additionally, Bitcoin's regulatory and technological risks, such as hacking and evolving government policies, are important considerations.

How Bitcoin Fits into a Diversified Portfolio

Many investors now view Bitcoin as part of a diversified portfolio. Some allocate a small percentage of their investment funds to Bitcoin, balancing its potential high returns with the stability of more traditional assets like stocks and bonds. Institutions like Tesla, Square, and MicroStrategy have also added Bitcoin to their balance sheets, showcasing its potential role as an alternative asset class.

Famous Investors and Their Views on Bitcoin

Prominent figures like Elon Musk, Jack Dorsey, and Cathie Wood are vocal proponents of Bitcoin. Their involvement has helped propel Bitcoin into mainstream investment discussions, driving awareness and interest in its potential. By studying their perspectives, readers can gain a sense of how major investors view Bitcoin as part of the future financial landscape.

With a clear understanding of Bitcoin as an investment, readers can consider how it might fit into their financial goals, weighing both the risks and rewards associated with this asset.

Chapter 10: Bitcoin and Financial Freedom

Bitcoin's potential extends beyond its status as an investment; it offers a unique pathway to financial empowerment and freedom. This chapter examines how Bitcoin can benefit individuals in regions with limited banking access, high inflation, or unstable governments.

The Potential for Bitcoin to Bank the Unbanked

According to the World Bank, over a billion people globally remain unbanked, without access to basic financial services. Bitcoin provides a solution, as it only requires an internet connection to transact. By using Bitcoin, individuals in underserved areas can store and transfer value, participate in commerce, and save money securely without needing a traditional bank account.

1.   Access Without Borders:
○   Bitcoin operates globally, enabling cross-border transactions without the high fees associated with international banks. For migrant workers, this means sending remittances to family members with lower costs and faster processing times.
2.   Financial Inclusion Through Technology:
○   In regions where mobile phone penetration is high but banking access is low, Bitcoin can bridge the gap. Users can store Bitcoin in digital wallets, offering a safe alternative to cash in areas with unstable currencies or limited infrastructure.

Bitcoin's Role in Countries with Hyperinflation and Financial Instability

In countries experiencing hyperinflation, such as Venezuela and Zimbabwe, local currencies lose value quickly, making everyday purchases difficult. Bitcoin, with its limited supply and decentralized nature, provides an alternative store of value that can protect against such economic crises.

1.   A Hedge Against Inflation:
○   Bitcoin's deflationary model and scarcity make it an appealing option in countries where fiat currency is rapidly losing value. As a digital store of value, Bitcoin can help individuals preserve wealth in times of financial turmoil.
2.   Empowering Individuals Against Financial Control:
○   Bitcoin's independence from government control means it cannot be devalued through excessive printing, making it a

potentially powerful tool for individuals in countries where the government controls or restricts financial access.

The Potential to Reshape the Financial System

Bitcoin represents more than a financial tool; it's part of a broader movement advocating for financial freedom and individual sovereignty. Advocates see it as a technology that can reduce dependency on centralized financial systems, offering people an unprecedented level of control over their own assets.

Chapter 11: Bitcoin's Environmental Impact

One of the most frequently discussed topics around Bitcoin is its environmental impact, particularly the energy-intensive process of mining. This chapter addresses these concerns, providing a balanced view of Bitcoin's energy use and the efforts being made to mitigate its footprint.

Bitcoin Mining and Energy Consumption: Facts vs. Myths

Bitcoin mining requires significant computational power to solve complex mathematical problems, a process that consumes large amounts of electricity. This energy consumption has led to concerns about Bitcoin's environmental sustainability. However, some points are often misunderstood:

1.   Energy Consumption vs. Environmental Impact:
○   Not all energy sources used in Bitcoin mining are harmful to the environment. Some mining operations rely on renewable energy, such as hydropower and solar power, especially in regions with surplus energy production.
2.   Comparing Bitcoin's Impact to Traditional Finance:
○   While Bitcoin's energy usage is high, it's essential to consider the energy costs of traditional financial systems, which include banking infrastructure, ATMs, physical currency production, and more. Bitcoin advocates argue that Bitcoin's energy footprint is relatively small in comparison.

Environmental Initiatives within the Bitcoin Community

In response to environmental concerns, Bitcoin miners and developers have taken steps to reduce the industry's environmental impact:

●   Shift to Renewable Energy: Many mining companies are moving to regions with access to renewable energy. Some estimates suggest that over 50% of Bitcoin mining already relies on renewable sources.
●   Carbon Offsetting Initiatives: Some organizations are exploring ways to offset Bitcoin's carbon footprint by investing in renewable energy projects and carbon capture initiatives.
●   Alternative Consensus Mechanisms: While Bitcoin remains committed to proof of work, some newer cryptocurrencies have adopted alternative models, like proof of stake, to reduce energy consumption.

Alternatives and Improvements in Energy-Efficient Mining

Advancements in mining technology are being made to increase efficiency. For instance, more energy-efficient hardware, known as ASICs (Application-Specific Integrated Circuits), has reduced energy use per transaction. Additionally, some developers are exploring the potential of second-layer solutions, such as the Lightning Network, to process transactions with minimal energy costs.

By understanding the nuances of Bitcoin's energy consumption and the efforts to reduce its impact, readers can make informed decisions about Bitcoin's environmental effects and consider potential future improvements.

Chapter 12: Future of Bitcoin

As Bitcoin continues to grow and evolve, many wonder what the future holds for this groundbreaking technology. This chapter explores potential challenges, technological innovations, and the role Bitcoin could play in the global economy.

Predictions for Bitcoin's Role in the Global Economy

Bitcoin's increasing adoption by individuals, businesses, and even governments suggests that it may become a significant asset in the financial world. Here are a few scenarios that experts anticipate:

1. Global Reserve Asset:
○   Some investors believe Bitcoin could serve as a global reserve asset, similar to gold. Its scarcity, portability, and resistance to inflation make it a potential hedge for countries and corporations alike.
2. Mainstream Adoption:
○   As more companies begin to accept Bitcoin for payments, it could become a widely used form of currency. Initiatives by

payment processors like PayPal and Square to integrate Bitcoin are early indicators of this trend.

3. Digital Financial Infrastructure:
○   Bitcoin's technology could inspire a wave of digital financial infrastructure that is decentralized and accessible globally, offering a future where people control their own wealth without relying on centralized banks.

Potential Challenges

1. Regulatory Hurdles:
○   Governments worldwide are considering stricter regulations on cryptocurrencies. While regulation could bring legitimacy, excessive control might stifle Bitcoin's decentralized nature and restrict its use in certain regions.
2. Technological Limitations:
○   Bitcoin's scalability is an ongoing concern. Current transaction speeds and fees could limit its use as a daily currency unless improved. Second-layer solutions like the Lightning Network aim to address this but are still developing.
3. Competition from Central Bank Digital Currencies (CBDCs):
○   Several countries are developing CBDCs—digital versions of fiat currencies issued by central banks. While different in purpose, CBDCs could compete with Bitcoin for public adoption, particularly in the realm of digital payments.

The Role of Bitcoin in the Future of Money and Finance

Bitcoin has already proven to be a disruptive force in finance, and it's likely to remain a key player in the digital economy. Whether as a store of value, a medium of exchange, or a financial tool, Bitcoin's influence on money and financial systems will be felt for years to come.

Chapter 13: Getting Started: Your First Bitcoin Purchase

This chapter offers practical, step-by-step guidance for beginners ready to make their first Bitcoin purchase. From setting up a wallet to securing funds, it covers the essentials to ensure a safe start in the world of Bitcoin.

Step 1: Setting Up a Bitcoin Wallet

Before purchasing Bitcoin, users need a secure wallet to store it. Here are the steps for setting up a basic wallet:

1. Choose a Wallet Type:
○   For beginners, software wallets (such as mobile or desktop wallets) are the most accessible. Popular wallets include Electrum, Exodus, and Mycelium.
2. Download and Install the Wallet:
○   Download the chosen wallet from a reputable source, either from an app store or the wallet's official website.
3. Secure the Wallet with a Strong Password:
○   Choose a strong, unique password and enable any available security features, such as two-factor authentication (2FA).
4. Back Up the Wallet:
○   Write down the recovery phrase (a series of 12-24 words) provided by the wallet. Store it securely, as this phrase is essential for recovering your Bitcoin if you lose access to the wallet.

Step 2: Buying Bitcoin

To buy Bitcoin, users typically use a cryptocurrency exchange. Here's how to go about it:

1. Choose a Reputable Exchange:
o   Platforms like Coinbase, Binance, and Kraken are popular for their user-friendly interfaces and security. Verify the exchange's reputation and fee structure before signing up.
2. Complete Identity Verification:
o   Most exchanges require users to complete a Know Your Customer (KYC) process, which involves providing identification and contact information.
3. Fund the Account:
o   Link a bank account, credit card, or another payment method to fund the exchange account. Be aware that some payment methods may incur higher fees.
4. Place an Order:
o   Once funded, you can place a "buy" order for Bitcoin. Specify the amount you want to purchase and review the transaction details before confirming.

Step 3: Transferring Bitcoin to Your Wallet

After buying Bitcoin, it's recommended to transfer it to a personal wallet rather than leaving it on the exchange for security purposes:

1. Locate Your Wallet Address:
o   In your wallet, find the public address (often shown as a QR code or string of characters).
2. Initiate the Transfer:
o   Enter your wallet address on the exchange's withdrawal page, confirm the transaction, and wait for the Bitcoin to arrive in your wallet.

By following these steps, beginners can safely make their first Bitcoin purchase and start their journey in the world of cryptocurrency.

Chapter 14: Conclusion: Navigating the Future with Bitcoin

In this final chapter, readers are encouraged to reflect on Bitcoin's potential and the knowledge they've gained from this guide. The journey to understanding Bitcoin is ongoing, with continuous technological, economic, and regulatory developments. Here's a recap of key takeaways and a final message for the reader.

Summary of Key Takeaways

1.   Bitcoin's Revolutionary Potential:
o   Bitcoin is more than just a digital currency; it represents a movement toward financial autonomy, transparency, and innovation.
2.   Understanding and Using Bitcoin:
o   Readers have learned the fundamentals of how Bitcoin works, how to buy and secure it, and the regulatory landscape surrounding it.
3.   The Future of Bitcoin:
o   With potential applications in finance, technology, and social empowerment, Bitcoin's future remains full of possibility.

Final Thoughts on the Potential of Bitcoin as a Currency and Technology

Bitcoin offers a new way to think about money, challenging traditional ideas of value, control, and finance. It empowers individuals to take control of their financial futures and provides a solution to many systemic issues found in traditional banking and currency systems.

Encouragement to Keep Learning and Stay Informed

The world of Bitcoin and cryptocurrency is constantly evolving. Staying informed about regulatory changes, technological advancements, and market trends will help readers make the most of their Bitcoin journey. As with any investment or technology, continual learning is key to success.

Bitcoin Unlocked is just the beginning, and readers are encouraged to explore further, deepen their knowledge, and consider how Bitcoin might fit into their personal and financial goals.